~~Janet Sherblom~~

From

~~Marjorie ~~ ~~   ~~

November 30, 1992

THE JOY OF
TEDDY BEARS

TED MENTEN

PUBLICATIONS
INTERNATIONAL, LTD.

ISBN: 1-56173-271-0

Library of Congress Catalog Card Number: 91-61592

Photo credits:
Front and back covers: Siede Preis Photography
Russ Berrie and Company, Inc.: 76; **Burtess Photographics/Kaleb Designs:** 10, 45, 64, 65; **Celestial Seasonings:** 27; **Dakin, Inc.:** 83; **Lynton Gardiner:** 70; **Sam Griffith Photography:** 53 (bottom), 54 (right), 55; **Gund:** 16, 84, 85; **Dee Hockenberry:** 8, 74 (top); **Ho phi le:** 11, 29, 71, 73, 75; **Ted Menten:** 1, 5, 15 (top), 17, 19, 23, 24, 25, 26, 31, 33, 34, 35, 36, 37, 38, 39, 40, 41, 42 (center), 43, 46, 47, 52 (right), 57, 58, 59, 67, 74 (bottom), 77, 78, 81, 82, 85, 86, 87, 88, 89, 90, 91, 92, 93, 94, 95, 96; **Gary Nett/Bears by Nett:** 6, 22, 49; **North American Bear Co., Inc.:** 18, 54 (left & bottom), 80; **Jim Samere/Frannie's Teddy Bear Museum:** 15 (bottom), 20, 61, 71 (bottom); **Siede Preis Photography:** 4, 7, 28, 30, 32, 35 (right), 42 (right), 48, 50, 51, 52 (left), 53 (top), 56, 66; **Smithsonian Institution:** 9; **Tide-Rider, Inc.:** 79; **Paul Volpp:** 60, 62, 63, 68, 69, 72; **John R. Wright/Dolls, Inc.:** 12, 14.

Ted Menten is an accomplished designer, photographer, collector, bear maker, and writer. His many books on teddy bears include *The Teddy Bear Lover's Companion, The World According to Hug,* and *Teddy's Bearzaar.* His articles on collectibles appeared regularly in *Dolls* magazine as well as *Teddy Bear Review.* He also co-authored *The Complete Book of Teddy Bears.*

CONTENTS

THE JOY OF TEDDY BEARS

DEAR OLD TEDDY

On the front porch of a large frame house, the grandparents sit and watch their children and their grandchildren play in the yard. They marvel at the wonder in their lives, remembering the good times and the bad, the hard times and good fortune, as they peacefully gaze out at the joys that time has brought to them. Looking back over the years, they hold hands, content simply to sit together and remember.

Up in the attic, the afternoon sun filters through the shutters, turning the cobwebs to spun gold. Amid the clutter—two unmatched high-button shoes, a victrola, an iron lamp with a beaded shade, and countless boxes of unnamed memories—the light falls on an old teddy bear. Once he was the dearly loved companion of the man the children downstairs call Grandpa. Now, his fur is tattered, one ear hangs by a few threads, and his belly sags in a paunch. His black shoe-button eyes remain bright, and he smiles a warm smile. He, too, is content to sit and remember.

above

TREASURE TED BY Linda Spiegel of Bearly There has been designed of distressed gold mohair. He has a black stitched nose and antique shoe-button eyes. Although more than just a bit tattered and worn, this charming bear is filled with love and no doubt carries hundreds of memories.

opposite page

CREATED BY Bonnie Wass McCabe, Rags stands 15 inches tall. Sitting among the shadows of the attic, this plush teddy wears a bright patchwork bow that might have been fashioned by someone's Granny on a long summer day. As night falls, this sweet bear will rest on his quilt and hope for a clear moon and a starry sky.

THE JOY OF TEDDY BEARS

FOREBEARS

The morning of November 13, 1902, was brisk. President Theodore Roosevelt was in Mississippi on a hunting trip, and the press followed his every move. After a fruitless morning, the president returned to camp for a hot lunch. Word soon came that a bear had been cornered, and Roosevelt quickly made his way to the scene. On arriving, he found the quarry, an injured bear that had been run all day by the dogs and was now roped to a tree. Moved by the creature's plight, TR refused to shoot the bear and ordered that it be humanely put out of its misery.

Back in Washington, D.C., a political cartoonist named Clifford Berryman heard the story and got an idea for a cartoon. He used the incident to illustrate the president's role in an ongoing state boundary dispute. The cartoon bear was immensely popular, and Berryman used the now-famous cub in many cartoons about Roosevelt throughout his presidency. America's love affair with "Teddy's Bear" had begun.

above
THIS TEDDY BEAR stands 18 inches tall. Created by Bill and Ilene Strauss, this teddy is all dressed up to take a ride with the famous regiment of Rough Riders.

opposite page
MR. TEDDY ROOSEVELT BEAR is 18 inches tall and made of silver-grey mohair. Created by Gary and Margaret Nett, he wears a traditional wool morning suit, cotton shirt, black silk tie, and black top hat. He also wears the unmistakable wire frame glasses of the man for whom he was named.

THE JOY OF TEDDY BEARS

While there is some question over the teddy bear's origin, it is very possible that Rose and Morris Michtom were the first to make and sell stuffed bears. Reportedly, Morris suggested the idea to his wife after seeing the famous cartoon about Teddy Roosevelt's hunting trip reprinted in the *New York Herald*. Some accounts even have the Michtoms writing to the president for permission to call their creation "Teddy's Bears." The president is said to have humbly allowed it, responding that while he didn't see the value in using his name, he also saw no harm in it. However, no such letters have ever been found to substantiate the story.

The Michtoms' first bears were about two-and-a-half feet tall and had shoe-button eyes. They were sold in the couple's sweet shop. Soon after, the Michtoms founded a new business, the famous Ideal Toy Company, and they began to mass produce the stuffed bears. In the years to come, this family business would manufacture a great many of America's best-loved toys. One of the original Ideal teddy bears now makes its home in the Smithsonian Institution in Washington, D.C.

above
THIS IDEAL BEAR has established a place in U.S. history for himself. Among the first teddy bears produced in this country, he currently resides at the Smithsonian Institution as a representative of one aspect of American culture.

opposite page
THIS EARLY IDEAL TEDDY is an example of the distinctive style of America's first teddy bear manufacturer. Standing ankle-deep in a snowbank, he is dressed in a plaid wool sweater and suede boots.

THE JOY OF TEDDY BEARS

In Giengen, Germany, toy maker Margarete Steiff was introduced to the idea of producing a jointed stuffed bear toy by her nephew Richard in the early 1900s. As a child Margarete had been stricken with polio and was confined to a wheelchair. While still a young girl, she opened her first dressmaking business. During the 1880s, she took the business in a new direction by beginning to manufacture stuffed toys, and Richard joined the company in 1897. He had been an art student in Stuttgart and had always loved drawing animals. He designed a toy bear that was jointed so that children could dress it and play with it like a doll.

Margarete did not like Richard's idea, but she made a prototype to please her nephew. In 1903 Steiff sent the jointed bear to the Leipzig Trade Fair with samples of their other toys. As Margarete expected, European buyers gave the bear a lukewarm reception, but an American distributor bought 3,000 of them and soon doubled the order. By the end of that year, Steiff had shipped more than 12,000 jointed bears to the United States, and they quickly became the most popular toy of the era.

above
STEIFF created this delightful 20-inch bear in 1909. This beautiful, nearly flawless teddy has the kind of heart-tugging expression that made these creatures so well-loved when they were first introduced and that continues to make them well-loved today.

opposite page
THIS "SPELLING TEDDY" was created by Steiff in 1904. Made of mohair and stuffed with excelsior, he has felt paw pads and boot-button eyes. This old teddy bear is in flawless condition and serves as a perfect example of the art of bear making as it was first practiced.

THE JOY OF TEDDY BEARS

LITERARY BEARS

In the early 1900s, teddy bears became a popular subject for children's books. One of the first stories to capitalize on the phenomenon was *The Roosevelt Bears*, which told the stories of Teddy B. and Teddy G. Since then, teddy bears have starred in countless books and comic strips.

No bear in the history of world literature is more beloved than Winnie-the-Pooh. The wonderful poems and stories that A.A. Milne wrote about his son's teddy bear have been translated into dozens of languages. The warmth, innocence, and loving nature that characterizes Pooh Bear may be the perfect personification of the teddy bear. Another British bear, Paddington, also became internationally famous. He is a charmingly muddled bear who has starred in several books and a television series. In the 1920s, Rupert appeared in the London *Daily Express*. This snow-white bear in yellow and black trousers and a red sweater was so popular that he became known as the British Mickey Mouse.

above
WHILE CLIFFORD BERRYMAN was the first cartoonist to create a popular version of the teddy bear, he was by no means the only one. Another important contributor to Teddy's early popularity was Seymour Eaton, who created Teddy B. and Teddy G., *The Roosevelt Bears*. These lovable characters appeared in both newspapers and storybooks.

opposite page
WINNIE-THE-POOH is far and away the most famous stuffed bear in the world. R. John Wright has created several adorable versions of Pooh and his friends that are closely modeled after Ernest Shepard's original drawings in the books by A.A. Milne.

Two more versions of Winnie-the-Pooh faithfully crafted by R. John Wright. The 18-inch Pooh *(above)* is supposedly a "life-size" version: the dimensions were calculated using drawings from the book and the average size of a child at Christopher Robin's age. Another Pooh *(right)* indulges in his favorite sport, honey snacking. This one comes complete with a blue-striped bib and his very own carefully labeled Hunny pot.

THE JOY OF TEDDY BEARS

right: ANOTHER FAMOUS AND ADORABLE TEDDY from England is Paddington. This fellow was found wandering the cavernous waiting room of the British train station he was named for. Dressed in this familiar garb and wearing a luggage tag with a message that no one could refuse, he found his way into the hearts of millions. This Paddington by Eden Toys has a tiny music box in the tummy, and his head moves in time to the tune.

left: RUPERT has been cavorting on the pages of the *London Daily Express* since 1920. In England, Rupert is as well-known as Mickey Mouse and Snoopy are in America. This version by Bradley & Ryan Imports stands 18 inches tall. He is made of soft white plush and wears the red, yellow, and black outfit that has been Rupert's trademark for decades.

THE JOY OF TEDDY BEARS

When Peggy and Alan Bialosky put their favorite bear on the cover of their catalog, they never could have guessed how well-loved he would become. Since the early days of his popularity, Bialosky Bear has been produced by Gund in a variety of styles and sizes. The pictured bears are special editions dressed in the same outfits as the original Bialosky.

THE JOY OF TEDDY BEARS

In recent years, many bears have become popular both as characters in books and as lovable, plush teddies. Some of them began their lives in storybook pages and later became real teddy bears. Others started out as cuddly stuffed toys and ended up having their lives depicted in words and drawings. All of them, though, are treasures that have been created for millions to enjoy.

Michele Clise has written several books about Ophelia, one of her much-loved Steiff bears. Ophelia is a Parisian shop girl, and her adventures have taken her to distant parts of the world. Steiff has recreated the original Ophelia and also makes teddies that have been inspired by other characters in the Ophelia books. The North American Bear Company has created a bear named Albert who has had several books written about his adventures. Bialosky Bear, manufactured by Gund, owes his origin to the publishing world, too. He first appeared on the cover of a teddy bear price guide compiled by Peggy and Alan Bialosky. A bear named Hug first appeared as a drawing in *The Teddy Bear Lovers Catalog*. Hug now has his own book and a whole line of plush bears.

OPHELIA is a 17-inch, fully jointed bear made from fine imported mohair. The original Ophelia is an antique Steiff bear that her owner, Michele Clise, featured in her books. Steiff has reissued this exquisite young bear, complete with a dainty lace collar and long, flowing pink ribbon, to commemorate her many exciting adventures.

ALBERT THE RUNNING BEAR began his life as a plush teddy
created by designer Barbara Isenberg for her son Christopher.
Soon afterward, the North American Bear Company was formed
and Albert could be found all across the United States. Today,
he is produced in several different sizes, has his own girlfriend
bear, and has become the hero of several children's books as
well as an exercise book.

THE JOY OF TEDDY BEARS

left: BABY HUG, designed by Ted Menten for the North American Bear Company, is the baby-size, cuddly version of the popular comic strip character Hug. Made of soft, particularly squeezable plush, this pint-size version of the philosophical grown-up bear was created especially for young children and adults with young hearts.

right: HUG is a comic strip bear who always manages to stay just one step ahead of trouble and winks his way through life with the philosophy that "it is the ambition of teddy bears to inspire love." This 18-inch, fully jointed plush Hug from the North American Bear Company was designed by the strip's creator, Ted Menten.

As often happens to teddy bears in real life, the fictional teddy Aloysius in Evelyn Waugh's *Brideshead Revisited* had been more or less forgotten over the years. When the novel was filmed for a British television series, a prominent role was written for Aloysius, and a casting call went out for old bears to play the part. Peter Bull, a famous character actor, author, and longtime arctophile, showed up with several of his favorite teddies who were eager for a chance to get into show business. A much-loved bear named Delicatessen was given the part of Aloysius.

After the series aired on television in Europe and later in the United States, the adorable old bear became an international star. He legally changed his name to Aloysius, and British Airways insisted that he fly first class when he came to visit America. After his companion Peter Bull died, the Nisbet Company made a perfect replica of Aloysius. The bear is made of distressed mohair and comes with a scarf and his own flight bag. The Nisbet company also makes Bully Bear, who is the hero of several of the books written by the late Peter Bull.

above
THIS PORTRAIT from the BBC television show *Brideshead Revisited* shows Delicatessen starring in the role of Aloysius, along with his costars Anthony Andrews *(left)* and Jeremy Irons *(right)*.

opposite page
THE REAL DELICATESSEN now resides in Frannie's Teddy Bear Museum. This same-size version is produced by Nisbet. He comes complete with his own British Airways flight bag and wears a distinctly British wool scarf around his neck.

THE JOY OF TEDDY BEARS

22

BEARS AT WORK

From the time the first teddy bear was created, all teddies have taken on the vital task of serving as loving and loved companions for children. Even in the early days, though, these sweet creatures were able to make a name for themselves in the business world. Perhaps the first real job given to teddy bears put them out on the campaign trail for President Theodore Roosevelt, who was running for a second term.

Teddy was remarkably successful in helping Roosevelt win reelection, and since that time many different companies have asked him to be their spokesbear. Teddy has endorsed all kinds of products from honey to automobile tires. He has spent countless hours posing for photographers and artists who have put his likeness in newspapers and magazines and on advertisements, premiums, logos, and packaging. Most recently, a charming little bear named Snuggle has been prominent in the advertising industry as the representative of a fabric softener.

above
LIGHTS! CAMERA! ACTION! This familiar character is a famous TV personality created by Russ Berrie. As the spokesbear for Snuggle Fabric Softener, this cute little fellow has made his way to the top of the advertising industry. Snuggle stands 15 inches tall and is covered in soft lamb's wool plush.

opposite page
THIS 18-INCH ROUGH RIDER by Gary and Margaret Nett would have been a persuasive representative for Teddy Roosevelt except that he's a good bit too large. The bears actually used in TR's bid for reelection were tiny ones that hung from campaign buttons.

THE JOY OF TEDDY BEARS

Many teddy bears have put their charm and lovability to use in supporting good causes. Smokey the Bear has been helping people prevent forest fires since the 1940s. He has been the center of one of America's longest-lived and most successful public relations campaigns. The United States government has been so pleased with his work that in 1984 he was given his own postage stamp as a birthday present. Smokey first appeared as a drawing on a poster, but he has since been produced in plush form by many companies.

No other spokesbear has had the impact of Smokey, but there are other bears who are working to save the environment and to make the world a better place to live. Determined Productions supports the World Wildlife Fund by contributing part of the money they make from selling teddy bears (and other stuffed animals) to the fund. Good Bears of the World is devoted to seeing that sick and distressed children the world over have teddy bears to offer comfort and companionship, and countless teddies have been donated and sold to raise money for BearAid, Save the Children, the Ronald McDonald House, and many other charities.

above
DETERMINED PRODUCTIONS employs a line of plush animals that help to raise money and increase awareness for the World Wildlife Fund, which helps endangered animals around the globe. The Grizzly Bear on the left is about 16 inches tall and his pal the Giant Panda is about 14 inches tall.

opposite page
FOR OVER FORTY YEARS, Smokey the Bear has been working to prevent forest fires and to help both children and adults nurture a respect for our national parks. This 12-inch Smokey sternly reminds all that "Only you can prevent forest fires."

Teddy recently has begun a new adventure. He has gone to work helping police departments comfort abused children. A familiar, huggable friend can be an eloquent translator between a terrified child and a concerned adult. Many teddy bears are at work in police and fire department trauma centers, in hospitals, and in classrooms. In the hospital, a special bear named Sir Koff-a-Lot encourages patients recovering from surgery to do the coughing needed to heal them. Other bears are regular visitors to nursing homes. Visits by these adorable, loving teddies can do a great deal to help brighten the days of the elderly patients there.

Many teddies accompany people to their jobs every day, where they wait patiently to listen to the day's frustrations, to help solve a special problem, or just to offer a brief respite from the pressures of the workday. Some bears may find their work in baby's crib and others may go out in the business world, but all teddy bears are the keepers of secrets and dreams. They have a job to do, and they are always willing to carry it out because every teddy is part of a long tradition of patience and love.

above
CELESTIAL SEASONINGS, the tea company, provides a generous service through their Best Buddy program. The company sends teddies out and puts them to work with law enforcement officers to help with the difficult task of calming and comforting distressed children.

opposite page
MUFFIN ENTERPRISES has created Sir Koff-a-Lot, a doctor's helper who works to prevent respiratory infections. He encourages patients recovering from chest or abdominal surgery to cough and clear their lungs despite the discomfort or unease it can cause.

THE JOY OF TEDDY BEARS

LITTLE BEARS

❦

During the late 1970s, miniatures of every kind suddenly became popular. Many people built doll houses and model railroads. Armies of tin soldiers stormed the battlements of tiny castles. Shops selling plans and supplies for scale models opened in many cities and towns, and television talk-show hosts tried to explain why building tiny domains was an appropriate response to the stressful world in which we live. Our friend Teddy found himself right in the middle of this craze for things small.

Some tiny teddies took their places beside the dolls' dolls in miniature nurseries, but other little bears made their way in the world on their own. Some of these little bears decorate hats, ride on the lapels of suit jackets and bathrobes, or swing from trapezes over babies' cribs. Others hide patiently in desk drawers or ride on car dashboards. As pocket bears, they can be found with adults and children almost anywhere that their owners' lives take them.

above

MINIATURE BEARS have been around for a good long time. This short fellow with the long face was produced by Steiff back in the 1950s. He stands only four huggable inches tall.

opposite page

THESE CREATIVE BEARS are the inspiration of Cleo Marshall, and they all measure under three inches tall. Made of velvet upholstery fabric and displaying amazing dexterity, they make a remarkable group of tiny Rembrandts.

IT's SLUMBER TIME for these two little Sandy Fleming teddies, so they've slipped on their favorite nighttime attire. Their crib may be quite tiny, but the bears will have plenty of room to move around and make themselves comfortable: Each measures less than two inches high.

THE JOY OF TEDDY BEARS

left: THIS MINIATURE BEAR was lovingly crafted by the hand of Kimberly Port and outfitted in an exquisite gown that could well be a Paris original. It's hard to say which is a greater work of art—the beautiful little bear or the delicate, lacy costume.

right: BOB CUBILLAS has created three amazing little bears that each has a personality of its own. Measuring under two inches tall, they are fully jointed and very posable. Fashioned of upholstery fabric that gives a furry look, these bears all wear gold stars around their necks.

During the 1920s, many companies produced small teddy bears, including some that were less than three inches tall. Schuco was well known for their tiny bears, and Schuco miniatures are now highly prized by collectors. Today, it is almost impossible to find a jointed manufactured bear that is shorter than five inches. But there are many teddy bear artists who specialize in tiny teddies, some no bigger than a thumbnail. When these specialists arrive at a teddy bear show with a hatbox containing the product of months of hard work, they are usually swamped with arctophiles who are eager to buy their little bears.

The tiny, portable bear is a miracle of ingenuity and craftsmanship. Imagine the effort that is required in creating a teddy as small as a half-inch high, with jointed arms and legs and a head that turns from side to side. Some bears are so small that they have to be seen under a magnifying glass in order for their beauty and fine detail to be truly appreciated. Crafting such a delicate work and imbuing it with the same loving cuddliness of a traditional teddy demands great patience and dedication.

above
BIG BROTHER and little brother stand tall at three and two-and-a-half inches. Created in tan alpaca by Grandma Lynn Lumley, this whimsical pair of cuddlesome cubs seems to cry out for someone to love and cherish them.

opposite page
MINIATURES from Hope Hatch, each wearing its own distinctive neckwear, make themselves at home in the kitchen. These bears are made from either Ultrasuede, floral print, or gold lamé, and some of them actually have jointed knees.

right: THESE SOFT, FUZZY miniatures come from the talented hand of artist Shirley Howey. Each acrobatically inclined five-inch bear wears a uniquely designed collar ribbon, and they come in a variety of lush colors.

left: HERE IS AN EXCEPTIONAL little teddy, only two-and-a-half inches high, from April Whitcomb. He looks like a miniature stuffed bear, but he is actually sculpted of plastic clay and then lovingly covered in velvet. He has a hand-painted face and comes housed in his own fabric-covered box.

THE JOY OF TEDDY BEARS

right: A TINY TEDDY DANCES his way from key to key as he types. Less than three inches high, he is made of white velvet upholstery fabric and has a black stitched nose. The little charmer was made by Cleo Marshall.

left: BY THE SEA, by the beautiful sea . . . sits a bear who has an ear tuned for the sound of the ocean's roar. This three-inch cub is the creation of Sue Newlin, and he is made of tan plush with matching felt paw pads.

THE JOY OF TEDDY BEARS

THE JOY OF TEDDY BEARS

36

BRING IN THE CLOWNS

If teddy bears have human counterparts who share their special way of showing love and joy, then these people are clowns, as we call them today. Clowns have a long and proud history that extends back through the courts of Europe to the time when the pharaohs ruled Egypt. Clowns have always helped us laugh; they show us the ridiculous in order to take our minds off the serious. Teddy bears, too, are there to make us smile and to give us welcome relief from the things that trouble us.

A simple pratfall or a perfect tumble from the nursery shelf will always get Teddy a big laugh, but give him the right costume and he becomes the noble fool. Some teddy bear artists create elaborate clown bears with colorful fabrics, carefully crafted accessories, and dyed fur, but a simple lace clown's ruff is often enough to transform an otherwise somber teddy into a playful little fool. Whatever the costume, all teddies seem well at ease when they're spreading joy.

above

DRESSED IN A BRIGHT BLUE polka-dotted net ruff trimmed in gold braid, this 14-inch mohair clown bear is the creation of Sheri Fickes. At heart, every bear is a bit of a clown, and this fellow proves that it only takes a colorful collar and a loving expression to put a smile on anyone's face.

opposite page

THESE 12-INCH WOOLEN JESTERS are dressed in pink and purple satin outfits trimmed with an explosion of lacy ruffles. Accented heavily with ribbons and bells, these two elegant clowns are the creation of Joanne Purpus and Cheryl Lyndsey, working together in a whimsical duet.

THESE TEDDIES BY STEIFF are reproductions of Steiff bears originally produced in 1913. Their subtle design and haunting, forlorn expressions make them timeless classics. Twelve inches tall, jointed, and made of mohair, they have bright colors and prominent neckbands that are somehow reminiscent of an old-time circus.

THE JOY OF TEDDY BEARS

left: THIS ENDEARING LITTLE BEAR by Gloria Rosenbaum seems to be crying on the inside. Wearing a blue collar trimmed in gold, she personifies all that is touching about clowns.

right: DRESSED IN AN ELEGANTLY CLOWNISH SUIT, trimmed with lace and silver bells, this bear by Beverly Port retains a certain dignified air about him. Standing 17 inches tall and made of mohair, he contains a music box that, appropriately enough, plays the tune "Be a Clown."

Teddy bears are adept at seizing the opportunity to become anything any child has ever loved. They like to dress up in old baby clothes and silly hats to make us happy, but almost every teddy seems to be especially pleased to don a jester's motley and make us smile at his own expense. The jester's costume, or motley, was a mockery of the current fashion trend in court. Its outlandish mix of garish colors and ornate trimmings was intentionally overdone to evoke a laugh. The fool's cap with its two or three points was oversized and floppy and made even more ridiculous by the addition of tiny tinkling bells. To complement the ridiculous garb, jesters usually carried a bauble, or marotte, a small staff topped by a head that was designed to look like the fool himself.

The original intent of a fool's motley was to mock the wearer and to make him look ridiculous, and the costume still works today. When Teddy puts one on, though, the chuckles he draws are always full of loving warmth. Even when he's wearing such a silly outfit, his soft, tender nature and his quiet strength seem to shine right through.

above
DRESSED IN MULTICOLORED metallic fabrics that would be fit for any jester, this 12-inch, mohair clown bear is the work of Donna Hodges.

opposite page
THIS TEN-INCH WOOL JESTER is decked out in purple brocade and velvet with a green and blue satin cap and curled slippers to match. This delightful little bear was created by Sylvana Jean Anderson.

left: THIS BRIGHT-EYED WOOL TEDDY is dressed in regal blue crushed velvet, striped French ribbon, antique lace, and intricate gold braid and bells. His matching marotte reflects the same mood. Created by Doris King, this ten-inch Elizabethan-style jester would be at home in any royal court.

right: THIS STATELY JESTER REFLECTS the colors and mood of the Venetian court during the Romanesque period. Created by Nona Wooley and standing 15 inches tall, he is dressed in noble tones of blue and burgundy. He carries a silver bauble and sports a distinctive black felt hat trimmed in ribbons and rosettes.

right: WITH FUR DYED DARK ROSE and evening blue, this 13-inch merry-maker completes his costume with golden bells and satin ribbons and bows. Crafted in ivory plush, he is the imaginative expression of artist Christine Shelters.

left: THE PERFECT ROYAL FOOL for the holiday season, this 18-inch mohair Christmas Jester was crafted by Dee Hockenberry. Dressed for the season in red and green, this dandy has a wee companion who sits on his shoulder and whispers holiday wishes into his ear.

Many teddy bears like to dress up as Harlequin. He was a famous character in the eighteenth-century Italian *commedia dell' arte,* and since then he's become a world-famous clown. He always wore the same type of costume and covered his face with a mask. Dressed in multicolored patchwork tights and a matching jacket, Harlequin looks somewhat like an elegant jester. Actually, he was probably one of the very first slapstick comedians. Harlequin never spoke or made a sound. Instead he used a bop on the head, a swift kick in the pants, or even a pie in the face to get across what he wanted to say as eloquently as any speech ever could.

Teddy seems to be very well suited to wearing the Harlequin's outfit because he brings his own special character to it. The soft, loving image created by a teddy bear is very different from that of the first Harlequin. The original was a buffoon and an outlandish prankster, but Teddy will always look strangely sad and especially huggable when he puts on this costume. Perhaps that's the very thing that makes a Harlequin teddy bear so endearing.

above
MUSICAL CLOWN COMES FROM the imagination of Barbara Wiltrout for Kaleb Designs. This 28-inch, hand-dyed bear is made of curly mohair and contains a music box. The Swiss-made, key-wound box plays "Send in the Clowns."

opposite page
BONNIE WAAS MCCABE has created a delightful pair of acrylic plush teddy clowns that are a playful study in black and white. The bright red pom-poms make an eye-catching accent to their costumes.

THE JOY OF TEDDY BEARS

WELL-DRESSED BEARS

Many people who love and collect teddy bears are purists. They like their bears to be bare, and they shun any garb more elaborate than a simple bow around the bear's neck. Other arctophiles provide their bears with a basic, simple wardrobe that might include a sweater, a T-shirt, overalls or a pinafore, and perhaps a few different hats. Some owners like to dress their bears in real children's clothes. An old teddy is proud to wear a hand-knit sweater or a smocked and embroidered dress that once belonged to his or her original owner.

Fashion has almost always been a part of Teddy's life. Soon after teddy bears were first introduced, magazines carried patterns for bear rompers, pinafores, sailor suits, party dresses, and nightshirts complete with slippers and caps. Today many successful bear makers feel that a teddy bear can become anything you can imagine if you only dress him appropriately. These people have made dressing teddies a new art form.

above

COMPANION STANDS 26 inches tall and is made of wavy mohair with Ultrasuede paws. Created by Ted Menten, this sweet-faced little girl bear is dressed in a rosebud print child's romper and carries her constant companion, a country bunny dressed in a matching outfit.

opposite page

AHOY LANDLUBBERS! This little sailor bear is shipshape and ready to heave anchor. Created by Judy Hill and standing 21 inches tall, this sea-going teddy wears a classical middy blouse complete with navy patch and red kerchief. He is made of long, shaggy mohair and has brown eyes and a hand-stitched nose.

left: BEVERLY WHITE has crafted three 11-inch teddies with a patriotic theme. Each soft wool bear has a stitched nose and mouth and represents a famous character in American history. On the left is Betsy Bear with her version of the first flag. In the center is Ben Bear, holding the familiar kite and key. On the right stands Thom Jefferson Bear, who holds a quill pen and a copy of the Declaration of Independence.

right: HONORING ENGLAND's royal traditions, this Beefeater stands 15 inches tall and is the work of Flore Mediate. He is made of white plush and dresses in the age-old red and black uniform of the royal guard, topped off with an authentic hat and staff.

THE JOY OF TEDDY BEARS

Many teddies wear simple, common outfits that could be a standard part of almost anyone's wardrobe, but there are other bears who are most comfortable in very unusual garb that you just don't see every day. These teddies draw on a wide variety of sources to find inspiration for the special clothes that they wear.

Some teddy bears, for example, have found places in the pageant of history. They dress as Union or Confederate soldiers, Revolutionary War heroes, Betsy Ross, or other famous figures from America's past. Others go to foreign countries and back to even more distant times, dressing in an English Beefeater's uniform, the armor of a heroic medieval knight, the timeless finery of a Japanese nobleman, or the kilt of a Scottish Highlander. Teddies are sometimes costumed as familiar characters from fairy tales, such as Pinocchio and Little Bear Riding Hood. Other bears are decked out for the holidays. There are Santa Bears, elf bears, and teddies with reindeer antlers for Christmas. Bears in bunny costumes or frilly bonnets celebrate Easter, and Uncle Sam Bear raises the flag on the Fourth of July.

THIS CONFEDERATE soldier bear is the creation of Gary and Margaret Nett. Standing 18 inches tall and fashioned of silver and grey mohair, he is uniformed in the traditional grey of the Confederate army. All of his brass buttons and insignia are exact replicas of the original designs.

left: JOANNE ADAMS has crafted a delightful eight-inch storybook bear Called Bearther Goose. Made of brushed wool and wearing a matronly floral print dress accented with a matching hat, this tiny fable teller has a companion goose and a wicker basket filled with treats.

right: LITTLE BEAR PEEP hasn't quite lost all of her sheep; these three have remained behind. This enchanting little shepherdess, complete with a crook, was made by Joanne Adams and stands eight inches tall. Each little sheep wears its own golden tinkling bell so that if they do wander off they'll be easy to find.

THE JOY OF TEDDY BEARS

right: THIS NINE-INCH VERSION of the famous puppet Pinocchio is made of plush, not wood like the original. The work of Jody Battaglia, he does wear the traditional alpine shorts and suspenders and the adorable little cap. He is made of pine-colored plush, and his bright black button eyes twinkle behind his whimsical expression.

left: NINE-INCH LITTLE Red Riding Hood was created by Jody Battaglia. This sweet little bear wears the famous red hood and cape and a beautiful help-me-I'm-lost expression. She carries a finely crafted wicker basket, no doubt filled with goodies for her granny.

THE JOY OF TEDDY BEARS

THREE BEARS ready to celebrate their favorite holidays. Designed by Mary Ellen Brandt from white and autumn-haze mink, Brooke *(above, left)* rings in the new year. Bunny Bear *(above)* from Bearly There is the perfect companion on an Easter egg hunt. A bear reminiscent of Uncle Sam *(left)* eagerly awaits a Fourth of July fireworks display.

right: MARTHA FAIN honors the Christmas season with this mohair Santa bear dressed in a crimson velvet robe trimmed with real mink and caught around the waist with a matching sash. Bringing to mind an old-fashioned Yuletide, he carries a tiny teddy that will no doubt end up in the stocking of a deserving little cub.

left: THESE TWO BEARS prepare to partake in a Thanksgiving celebration. As a dedication to the courage and strength of the Founding Bears, they have dressed themselves in authentic, meticulously fashioned pilgrim outfits for the occasion.

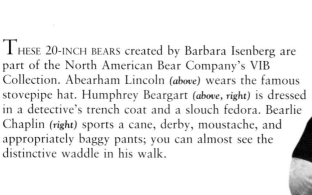

Tʜᴇꜱᴇ 20-ɪɴᴄʜ ʙᴇᴀʀꜱ created by Barbara Isenberg are part of the North American Bear Company's VIB Collection. Abearham Lincoln *(above)* wears the famous stovepipe hat. Humphrey Beargart *(above, right)* is dressed in a detective's trench coat and a slouch fedora. Bearlie Chaplin *(right)* sports a cane, derby, moustache, and appropriately baggy pants; you can almost see the distinctive waddle in his walk.

THE JOY OF TEDDY BEARS

When teddy bears first appeared, they were intended as children's toys, but as we all know they rather quickly worked their way into the hearts of many adults with their loving nature and their gentle compassion. In some ways, the clothes available to teddy bears have undergone a similar development. At first, the clothes were made as accessories for a child's plaything, but lately many of the fashions that have been designed especially for bears have a distinctly adult appeal to them.

One manufacturer has produced a sassy little cub with a flash of mischief in her eyes who dresses, appropriately enough, in a teddy, a silk and lace undergarment that was very popular in the 1920s and has made a strong comeback today. Another mature, but much less risqué, theme sets the tone for the imaginative outfits of the VIBs, or Very Important Bears, of the North American Bear Company. These colorful characters include such noted celebrities as Humphrey Beargart, Bearilyn Monroe, and Lauren Bearcall. All of these delightful bears wear specially designed outfits that are reminiscent of their namesakes.

CINDY LOU is a 17-inch teddy who wears a teddy. Tatum Egelin has crafted this little beauty of vintage materials; the shaggy fur that covers her used to be used to make imitation fur coats in the 1940s. Cindy Lou also wears a lovely rosebud band by her right ear.

left: Bᴀʀʀɪꜱᴛᴇʀ ʙᴇᴀʀꜱ have an eye for the right side of the law. Created by Sylvia Dombrowski, these 24-inch lawyers wear wool vests and carry leather briefcases. They look professional enough to make a guest appearance on *L.A. Paw* or *Bearry Mason.*

right: Wᴇꜱᴛᴡᴀʀᴅ Hᴏ! This 18-inch plush cowbear named Clint is jointed and made of acrylic fur. The creation of Joyce Francies, he wears sheepskin chaps, a red leather vest, a felt hat, and a shining sheriff's badge.

THE JOY OF TEDDY BEARS

For many bears, getting dressed can be a rather serious business. These teddies have work to do, and the extravagances of comfort and personal finery simply have no place in their busy day. Instead of wearing the latest trends or paying homage to a beloved figure or a bygone era by donning special garments, they must dress themselves in the traditional uniforms that their professions require.

Teddies have been dressed to handle almost any job that you can think of. Some have worn the clothes of doctors, nurses, lawyers, and business people. Others have dressed as ballerinas and painters, gold miners and cowboys, astronauts and magicians, pilots and bellhops, farmers and bakers—the list goes on and on and on. The publication of *Teddy's Bearzaar* showed that teddy bears could become fashion models. In this satire of a popular fashion magazine, tall, thin teddy bears wear haute couture fashions by Yves Saint Bearent, Bearre Cardin, and Bearry Ellis. These bears also sport makeup by Elizabear Arden, and their fur is styled by José Ebear. Their perfumes come from Houbeargant and Glorious Vanderpelt.

THIS TOO-TOO CHIC bear by Mary Holstad is straight from the pages of *Teddy's Bearzaar*. She wears black silk lounging pajamas and a China red silk dressing gown, complemented by patent leather pumps and bright red earrings. This 16-inch white mohair bear represents the peak of teddy bear fashion.

CAPE CANABEARAL is an astronaut designed by Barbara Isenberg for the North American Bear Company. Standing 21 inches tall and made of chocolate brown plush, he's ready to travel the universe to seek out new life forms and new civilizations, to boldly go where no bear has gone before. Other artists have created teddies that Canabearal might meet on his journeys.

THE JOY OF TEDDY BEARS

right: MARCIA SIBOL created the Just Married couple from the Space Station Freedom. Hannibal wears his dress uniform of black and silver. His bride Hope wears a modern yet classical gown of silver metallic fabric accented with lace, silver braid, and soft ribbons. About her head she wears a star-studded silver veil.

left: STARCATCHER was created by Ted Menten and stands 15 inches tall. Acting as both an ambassador and guide to the universe, this captivating white bear has twilight blue eyes and a rosy embroidered nose. Dressed in shimmering metallic fabric and enwreathed by a circle of stars, he soars through the universe delivering his message of goodwill and love. This feather-light bear is filled with tiny air pellets, making him almost weightless and letting him travel with the speed of light.

THE JOY OF TEDDY BEARS

THE JOY OF TEDDY BEARS

60

BEARS IN MOTION

❦

Teddy bears first became active very early in their history. As long ago as 1907, bear makers were devising clever ways for Teddy to come to life. The first talking bears did not speak human language but growled appropriately. The first teddy that really communicated was the yes/no bear made by the German toy maker Schreyer and Company. This furry charmer has a mechanism connecting his tail to his head that allows him to nod and shake his head.

Old issues of *Playthings,* the trade journal of the American toy industry, are filled with ads for all kinds of active bears. There were bears on wheels, bears who beat drums, bears who did acrobatics and tumbled, and bears who opened their mouths to drink from bottles. The Electric Bright Eye Teddy Bear had eyes that lit up red or white when you shook his right paw. Some teddies could play a Strauss waltz when you wound up a music box in their backs. Other teddies were bankers who swallowed coins.

above

THIS 29-INCH honey-colored bear was produced by Steiff around 1907. In a way, he was one of the earliest talking bears. His tummy contains a growler that sounds off when the bear is turned upside down.

opposite page

MOKO is a mechanical dancing bear that performs his act with the help of a colorful circus clown. This 1920s wind-up toy is a charming example of simple ingenuity and whimsy. Then as now, a smiling clown and a dancing bear are all that's needed to make a young child laugh.

left: SCHUCO created this three-inch tumbling bear made of golden mohair with black shoe-button eyes and an embroidered nose and mouth. The bear was costumed in a felt suit and was loosely jointed so that he could easily flop over and tumble.

right: THIS SCHUCO TUMBLING BEAR uses his elongated arms to support himself while he swings his legs and body. Only two inches tall, he's an example of an extremely popular toy from Teddy's early days that was the delight of both children and adults.

THE JOY OF TEDDY BEARS

right: ANOTHER EXAMPLE OF Schuco's mechanical genius was this skating bear from 1924. Made of gold mohair and beautifully costumed in colorful felt with metallic trim, this wind-up bear took center rink every time.

left: THIS SCHUCO SKATING BEAR wears silver skates and carries a red wooden stick. He has black button eyes and an embroidered nose and mouth. First sold around 1912, he's shown here next to the delightfully illustrated box that he originally came in.

THE JOY OF TEDDY BEARS

LINUS stands 28 inches tall and is the creation of Barbara
Wiltrout. He is made of gold mohair and has brown eyes and an
embroidered nose and mouth. A yes/no bear, he contains a
mechanism that allows you to nod his head up and down or
shake it from side to side. Like any young cub, he usually says
yes to honey and no to bedtime.

THE JOY OF TEDDY BEARS

BEAR ON WHEELS IS 18 inches tall and 24 inches long. Created by Barbara Wiltrout, this mohair bear stands securely on metal axles with wheels on either end so that he can be pulled along by his bright red ribbon. This bear also has a very flexible jointed head that can move in virtually any direction at any angle.

THE JOY OF TEDDY BEARS

Everyone who has ever loved a teddy bear feels that somehow his or her bear is alive. Imagination animates all teddy bears, making them able to talk, smile, and hug, but some special bears can also walk, dance, and even move their lips when they talk. Today computer technology has brought new life to our old friends.

In the years since the first teddy with a voice box growled, there has been no dance step, popular song, or sports craze that Teddy has not mastered, with a little help from his friends. Today's mechanical bears do amazing tricks, but computer chips are making it possible for Teddy to do almost everything a child ever imagined him doing. Teddy Ruxpin is such a bear. He not only talks and sings, but he moves his eyes and mouth in perfect synch with his voice. This thoroughly modern bear has his own wardrobe, and many books have been written about his life. Teddy Ruxpin is special because he is *not* a traditional teddy bear. He appeals to today's children, who will probably have the same feelings about their old Teddy Ruxpins as people who grew up with Steiff bears have about their old teddies.

above

WHEN WORLDS OF WONDER introduced Teddy Ruxpin, he was an immediate sensation. Not only could he speak in a clear, humanlike voice, but his eyes and mouth moved along with his words. He wasn't exactly cuddly, but his loving personality was so charming that children wanted him as a constant companion.

opposite page

ANN INMAN created this mechanical bear who has a magical crystal ball that lights up. Standing 26 inches tall and made of wool, this little magician contains a mechanism that moves his body and head in an extremely lifelike motion. He wears a sparkling silver and black wizard's robe and hat.

THE JOY OF TEDDY BEARS

Buying old bears

Antique dolls have long been the most highly valued old children's plaything, but today teddy bears are more and more often demanding the highest prices at auctions. Old dolls are considered most valuable when they are in mint, or nearly flawless, condition. Buyers like them to be as well preserved as possible. The recent jump in the prices paid for old teddy bears, though, has almost nothing to do with bears that are in mint condition.

Every teddy bear in the world is a unique character with its own smile, its own softness, its own personality. But all teddies have one thing in common: They were made to be loved. When a teddy has served for years as a loyal, loving companion, time and hugs can begin to take their toll. For many bear lovers, the perfect teddy is one that proudly displays its worn fur, its ragged smile, or its missing eye like a badge of friendship. The teddy who has been invested with thousands of hugs and kisses causes a clamor on the auction floor.

above
THIS SIX-INCH bear is dressed in the familiar tight-fitting jacket and flat pillbox hat of a bellboy. Produced by Schuco in the early 1900s, he is a yes/no bear, capable of shaking or nodding his head.

opposite page
BO IS A beautiful 24-inch bear created by Steiff in 1905. Made of golden mohair, he has a shaved muzzle with an embroidered nose and mouth. Bo is a flawless example of the center-seam style bears that are so popular with collectors today. The central gusset (the forehead and nose bridge) are two pieces of material stitched together instead of being made from the usual single piece.

THIS GROUP OF early teddy bears is enjoying a leisurely jaunt in
an antique pedal car painted a bright yellow with red racing
stripes. What a perfect way to spend an afternoon—a quiet drive
through the country in the company of good friends.

THE JOY OF TEDDY BEARS

right: B<small>Y</small> 1907, the teddy bear craze was in full swing in America as thousands of eager shoppers lined up to purchase a fuzzy friend for themselves or a loved one. Among the most popular manufacturers was the Ideal Toy Company, which may have created the first teddy bear. This 16-inch Ideal bear dates from 1907 and has the kind of charm that makes him an eye-catcher even today.

left: T<small>HIS CLASSIC BEAR</small> was manufactured by Tebro. He goes by the name of Rupert and currently resides in Frannie's Teddy Bear Museum as a representative of the early stages of the teddy bear's history.

THE JOY OF TEDDY BEARS

The true arctophile judges a teddy bear by the amount of loving wear his face and body display. Firm, evenly stuffed, unhugged teddies with perfect paws are less desirable than bears with sagging bellies, torn ears, and a missing eye. This teddy radiates the glow of love he has received over the years. A bear who has obviously been the keeper of a child's most cherished secrets seems to possess the same magical quality that makes people want to purchase old love letters and tintypes. Many of today's teddy bear artists have reconstructed this magic quality in the new bears they make by distressing them to give them a preloved look.

An antique by definition is something that is at least 100 years old. There will be no such thing as an antique teddy bear until the year 2003, when Teddy celebrates his centennial. Although most people don't adhere strictly to the definition of the word *antique* when it comes to teddies, old teddy bears are correctly called collectibles. Whatever their exact classification, wonderful well-loved teddies now bring high prices when they are placed on the auction block, often outpricing antique dolls.

above
By 1906, THERE were hundreds of companies, both American and European, producing thousands of teddies. This pale golden mohair bear stands 19 inches tall and was probably made in America.

opposite page
THE ADORABLE Happy Anniversary Bear is 24 inches tall and crafted of tipped mohair. Happy, as he is affectionately known, was produced by Steiff in 1926. In 1989, he was sold at auction for a record $86,350.

left: THIS STEIFF BEAR from around 1910 shares his chair with Treff, a Steiff dog who is a few years younger, and Pooh Bear the Cat, who is by far the youngest of the group. The 29-inch teddy is made of mohair and has felt paw pads.

right: THIS TINY TEDDY has served in the same family as a constant companion to three generations of gentlemen named Theodore. Today this pocket bear is called Grandpa, and he is a delightful teller of tall tales. Created by Steiff in 1907, he is made of gold mohair, is fully jointed, and has black button eyes and a meticulously embroidered nose and mouth. Grandpa has traveled around the world but still feels that there's no place like home.

THE JOY OF TEDDY BEARS

Out for a walk in the woods, this lovely bear is dressed in black pants and a dainty little bow tie and collar. Produced by Steiff in 1909, he stands 20 inches tall. He is covered in gold mohair, and his unforgettable expression is achieved with shoe-button eyes and embroidery for the nose and mouth.

THE JOY OF TEDDY BEARS

THE JOY OF TEDDY BEARS

MANUFACTURED BEARS

Teddy bears have been manufactured in factories since the time they first appeared. Originally almost all bears were made with mohair fur and stuffed with excelsior, a straw-like material that required repeated hugging and squeezing before Teddy developed into a soft, bunchy, comfortable bear. Over time, though, different materials and different methods have been used by manufacturers to create a variety of lovable, distinctive teddies.

Some companies make realistic teddies using synthetic fur that matches the colors of real bear fur; others make brightly colored bears that don't look anything like bears in nature. Some manufactured teddies are jointed and have movable heads, shoulders, and knees. Other bears aren't jointed so that every part of them has a soft, special cuddliness, while still others have flexible armatures that let them hold any pose. No matter what color their plush or where and how they were manufactured, all teddy bears are ambassadors of love.

above

THE CREATION of Sun and Star, Little Brown Bear is 15 inches high. He is a soft and cuddly plush unjointed bear with bright brown eyes who seems ready to reach out and give a hug to the whole world.

opposite page

THESE TWO So Soft Teddies were created by the Russ Berrie Company and are made of tan plush. They have bright brown eyes and rust-colored stitched noses. Each of these country-style bears wears a bright plaid ribbon, and the little guy seems to have a honey pot all his own.

left: STEIFF introduced this Clifford Berryman Bear in commemoration of the character that started the teddy bear craze back in 1903. Inspired by the now-famous cartoon and designed by Linda Mullins, this 14-inch fully jointed mohair bear is a delightful reminder of the teddy bear's roots.

right: WEARING ONE OF his owner's teddy bear ties, the Steiff limited edition Poppa Bear looks ready for any formal occasion. Standing 16 inches tall and made of imported gold mohair with matching felt paw pads, this distinctive bear has won the hearts of teddy bear collectors around the world.

THE JOY OF TEDDY BEARS

right: MERRYTHOUGHT is one of England's leading bear makers, and this 11-inch Elizabethan Bear is just one of the many charming teddies that they manufacture. This fully jointed teddy has brown eyes and a cute embroidered nose. Accented with a simple silk ribbon bow, this is a perfect first bear for a child of any age.

left: MERRYTHOUGHT created these two shaggy mohair bears and named them Wellington. Standing 15 and 21 inches tall and adorned with bright scarlet ribbons, these bright-eyed fellows have close-clipped muzzles and stitched noses.

Today millions of teddy bears are produced in factories. They are made in giant new factories in Korea, the original factories in Germany, and cottage industries in the United States, but even when teddies are mass produced no two teddies are exactly alike because there is no machine that can make a complete teddy bear. Machines cut out the pattern pieces from fur fabric, sew the pieces together, put on the eyes and noses, and even stuff teddy bears. But there is still a great deal of handwork required. Despite technological advances, teddy bears continue to be made today in much the same way that they always have. This human touch is part of what gives each teddy his own special personality.

When you go shopping for a bear, the shelves may seem to be filled with teddies who all look exactly alike. As you look at them more closely, you will see many differences. Eyes are set closer or wider apart, one ear is lopsided, a smile is crooked, or a mouth is slightly sad. Just like human beings, each bear is different. In time, each bear finds the right person to adopt him, and each person finds the right bear to love.

above
NORTH AMERICAN BEAR COMPANY has created a cute and cuddly version of the famous character Aloysius from the popular television show *Brideshead Revisited.*

opposite page
ONE OF THE MOST POPULAR BEARS created by the North American Bear Company is Muffy, the youngest cub in the Vanderbear family. Here, she is seen in one of her many costumes, a Western jumper with boots and a cowboy hat. She is accompanied by her pet horse Oatsie, who wears a matching bridle and halter. This is one of the cutest pairs you'll ever find riding the range.

left: LINDA SPEIGEL has designed these two Bunny Bears for her company Bearly There. They are fully jointed and made of soft tan plush with matching felt paw pads. In addition to the precious white bunny hat, each bear has a white fuzzy cotton tail in back.

right: GIDDYAP, HORSIE! This rocking bronco buster stands 14 inches high (out of the saddle) and was created by the Hermann Company in Germany. Made of soft mohair with felt paw pads, this cowteddy has brown eyes and an embroidered nose and mouth. Both he and his pony are accented in bright red.

THE JOY OF TEDDY BEARS

left: DAKIN presented this delightful little red plush bear named Bearistroika as an ambassador of peace and friendship. He wears a traditional Russian fur hat and a peasant shirt with embroidered trim. The display shows the familiar turrets found in Moscow's famous Red Square.

right: STRIKE UP THE BAND and let's have a parade. These colorfully dressed bears are the creations of the Dakin company. Made of long plush with dark-trimmed paws, they wear colorful costumes of bright fabric and ornate gold braid.

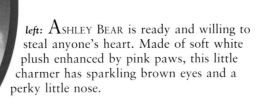

left: ASHLEY BEAR is ready and willing to steal anyone's heart. Made of soft white plush enhanced by pink paws, this little charmer has sparkling brown eyes and a perky little nose.

THE JOY OF TEDDY BEARS

CREATED BY GUND, these 17-inch floppy bears are made of fuzzy
beige plush with contrasting almond-colored trim and hand-
embroidered noses. Cute and cuddly, they answer to the name Wuzzy
and they're brightened by red plaid ribbons.

Teddies are produced in factories all over the world. From the very beginning, they have been an international phenomenon. The very first toy bears were made in Germany by Steiff and in the United States by the Ideal Toy Company. Steiff is still manufacturing teddy bears today, along with another German company that dates back to the turn of the century, Hermann, but Ideal has disbanded. England has also played a prominent role in Teddy's history. One British company, J. K. Farnell, has claimed that they actually created the first teddy.

Through the years, many other bear-making companies have also come and gone. Schuco, Knickerbocker, Dean's, Gebrüder-Bing, and Chad Valley used to manufacture many kinds of teddies, and most of them have now become treasured collectibles. Today, there are many manufacturers of fine bears that will no doubt be the collectible bears of the future. Nisbet, Gund, Dakin, and Merry-thought have been producing lovable teddies for many years. North American Bear Company, Russ Berrie, Applause, and many other companies began making wonderful bears in the 1980s.

GUND created this pair of oversized, cuddlesome bears named Baron. These two are 28 and 24 inches tall, and they have deep-set brown eyes and shaved muzzles. These bears share some unusual features. They have supple leather noses and a fine multi-filament plush covering that gives them a more natural, furry look.

THE JOY OF TEDDY BEARS

Handmade Bears

Not long after the first commercially manufactured teddy bears were adopted by American boys and girls, mothers and grandmothers began to make teddies at home. Patterns for bears and their clothes were sold through magazines and in dry-goods stores. Some people may have made teddy bears because they could not afford to buy them, but many people crafted bears because they wanted to give a child or a friend a special gift that was made with love.

Over the years, other toys captured the hearts of children. Grown-ups went along with the children's fancies and sewed all kinds of stuffed dolls and toys from Raggedy Ann to Cabbage Patch Kids. An interest in teddies was always there, though, and people continued to make them at home. As Teddy began to enjoy a resurgence in our hearts over the last 20 years, more and more teddies were created by hand. Today, there are hundreds of true artists who lovingly craft bears for the world to enjoy.

above

THIS CHARMING LITTLE GIRL BEAR, created by Jane Carlson, stands 13 inches tall and is made of imported gold mohair. She is elegantly dressed for travel in a royal blue velvet coat and matching hat, both trimmed with gold braid and buttons to match.

opposite page

BARBARA CONLEY has created a pair of off-white bears that seem to be perfect companions. Made of imported mohair, they stand ten and six inches tall. They have an air of Victorian elegance suggested by the oversized bow and the delicate amber shade of their noses.

This COUNTRY BEAR is 16 inches tall and made of fine imported mohair. She has bright brown eyes behind her gold-rimmed granny glasses. A fine lace trim accents both her dress of blue country print fabrics and her wide-brimmed straw hat. With this outfit, she seems ready to set out for the county fair or the weekly square dance. Bear artist Suzanne Tyler leaves her signature on this bear in the form of the painstakingly cross-stitched paw pads.

THE JOY OF TEDDY BEARS

left: THIS DELIGHTFUL 15-inch teddy has glass eyes and a golden-brown stitched nose. Made of long, thick, shaggy mohair, he sports a rainbow-striped French silk ribbon. This lovable, fuzzy-faced heartbreaker was created by Linda Suzanne Shum.

right: KIMBERLY HUNT designed this soft, fuzzy grey plush teddy who stands 12 inches tall and has matching Ultrasuede paw pads. His bright shoe-button eyes peek out from the fringe of his fur bangs, and his deep brown stitched nose sets off his smoothed snout.

THE JOY OF TEDDY BEARS

In the early 1980s gallery shows in New York, teddy bear stores in California, and the publication of many new books about old teddy bears encouraged more and more people to become bear makers. Today, hundreds of people make and sell stuffed bears. Their work is exhibited and sold at conventions, stores, and galleries all over the world, but more bear makers live and work in California and Washington than anywhere else. In 1990 the first teddy bear museums opened in Florida and Japan.

The challenge of bear making lies in coming up with a successful and original design. To create the bear that best expresses their idea of what a teddy should be, bear makers will endlessly experiment with patterns, stuffing materials, jointing systems, and fabric colors and textures. Many artists use traditional mohair, a fur fabric made from goat yarn that most teddies were made with at the turn of the century. Other people have extended the standard stock of teddy bear materials and taken the craft in a whole new direction. These bear makers incorporate wood, porcelain, metal, plastic, and even real fur in their teddies.

above

THIS CHUBBY 16-inch cream-colored plush teddy seems more than a bit absorbed in manipulating an intricate cat's cradle of red yarn. His wide-set brown eyes and prominent velvety nose give him the delightful expression of a young cub at play. Bear maker Judi Maddigan has created an irrepressibly huggable friend.

opposite page

THIS 11-INCH BEAR is covered in golden mohair fur. His shaved snout is set off by the wide black stitched nose. He seems to be right at home on this handmade, early American style patchwork quilt, which is also the work of his creator, Steve Schutt.

right: BEVERLY PORT has crafted a lovable teddy bear made of tan plush and felt paw pads. Standing 14 inches tall and wearing a loud plaid ribbon, this fellow wants to toot his own horn and make the world sit up and take notice.

left: AT EASE in the hands-behind-the-back pose that has become the trademark of artist Diane Gard, this golden mohair teddy stands 12 inches high. Wearing only a simple white silk ribbon, he displays a glass heart to show the world that, like all of Gard's creations, he is a "bear with a heart."

left: CORLA CUBILLAS was the maker of this 14-inch, champagne-colored mohair bear whose appointments all seem just a bit too big. The large glass eyes, the broad expansive stitched nose, and the overwhelming flowered bow give him a wistful, needy expression that can win over any heart.

right: CREATED BY SUE NEWLIN, this bear is 26 inches of warm shaggy plush accompanied by deep blue silk and outrageous red polka dots. His closely clipped face lets the friendliness and affection of his expression shine through.

THE JOY OF TEDDY BEARS

Making bears is a relatively new form of artistic expression. Most of the people who are now making teddy bears used to make dolls or other more traditional crafts, but some bear makers used to be painters, sculptors, or dressmakers. A few others actually began making their bears as a hobby. When they found how much pleasure their creations brought and how much love others felt for their work, they devoted their careers to spreading this special joy.

Anyone who is making a living by making teddy bears feels a strong sense of accomplishment, but there are also other ways in which excellence is recognized. At almost every convention that is held today, teddy bears are categorized and judged. While prizes are usually given for artistic merit to the Best Bears of Show, other categories are also given their due consideration. Awards are presented for such things as Most Hugged Bear, Most Elegantly Dressed Bear, Biggest Bear, and of course Smallest Bear. Each show sets its own standards and creates its own categories, but every teddy loves to bring home a blue ribbon for the artist who made him.

above

THIS ROSY, CREAMY BEAR by Ann Inman has mohair fur and felt paw pads and stands 11 inches tall. His bright black eyes sparkle gaily above a mouth that is just askew enough to make him completely irresistible.

opposite page

THIS GREY PLUSH BEAR wears soft brown trim in his ears and on his paw pads. Creator Jacquelyn L. Allen calls him her Black Forest Bear. He is 15 inches tall and wears a gold tinkling bell fastened with a subdued pink bow.

HE'S PIGEON-TOED, his bangs hang over his eyes, and his ears are unmistakably lopsided—in short, he's absolutely adorable. This 17-inch bear crafted by Ted Menten wears antique golden mohair and carries a beautiful heart trimmed in Victorian lace and filled with crushed dried roses.

THE JOY OF TEDDY BEARS